I Am Not a Juvenile Delinquent

I Am Not a Juvenile Delinquent

An anthology of poetry from the creative writing program at Touchstone

Edited by Sharon L. Charde

A residential treatment center for female juvenile offenders

Litchfield, Connecticut

Sharon Charde
Lakeville, CT 06039
Copyright © 2004 by Sharon Charde. All rights reserved.
Printed in the United States of America.

Book Designer: Virginia Anstett

"In My World" by Y. R. is forthcoming in *Women's Studies
Quarterly*, Vol. 33, nos. 3 & 4, Fall/Winter 2004, New York:
The Feminist Press at CUNY. Issue title: "Women, Crime
and the Criminal Justice System".

"My Kitchen Table" and "Smooth Pain" by T. R. appeared
in *Fresh Voices* 2001 (7 winners of the Young Poets
Competition, Sunken Garden Poetry Festival, Hill-Stead
Museum, Farmington CT 06032).

Library of Congress Control Number: 2004093515
ISBN Number: 0-9755366-0-5

Acknowledgements

This book is dedicated first of all to all the amazing, open-hearted, courageous young women who have been in my creative writing groups over the years I have worked at Touchstone. They have inspired me tremendously and pushed me to do things I never would have done without my drive to have their voices heard in this world. They have taught me about a different kind of living from that of my privileged society; they have brought color to my white universe. And, because of them, I can see my own long-ago adolescence through the prism of our shared experience, with compassion for all of us. I am so grateful to you, girls. And though I would love the world to know your beautiful names, the poems in this chapbook are published anonymously out of respect for your privacy.

Without the support of Program Director Michelle Sarofin and the staff at Touchstone, I would never be able to do this work. They have welcomed me into their midst and I so appreciate it. I am also grateful to former directors Lori Lalama and Meg Gleason who cheered me on despite their daily struggles with other aspects of the program. I am especially grateful to Lesley Murphy and Jennifer Block, former Touchstone staff members who gave me much-needed assistance with the girls and a great deal of their free time in so many ways. I am thankful also to Stewart Wilson of Artwell in Torrington who has hosted my girls for five wonderful public readings, as well as to the Brookfield Theatre for presenting our V-Day monologue in 2003 and their very generous contribution to Touchstone which will make more arts projects possible. I extend much gratitude to Nancy Gaynor, Nancy Bird and the young women of The Hotchkiss School in Lakeville, CT who have become a vital and thrilling part of creative writing by inviting us to join them once a month for dinner and a shared writing experience, as well as hosting two very successful readings at the school. Thank you also to Suzanne Heyd who invited the girls to her poetry class at Danbury High five years ago and gave us our first experience as guest readers – and this year invited us again to ALL Gallery in New Haven for another triumphant public appearance.

And then there are the women of Monday Poets as well as my other writing and non-writing friends who have steadily encouraged

me to do the work they can see brings me so much grati-
fication and joy; I thank you all, especially my dearest
friend Davyne Verstandig who has always understood. To
my husband John, a patient and constant sounding board
and support, another bouquet of large thank yous. All of
these nurturing and supportive connections have made
this book and my work at Touchstone, possible.

Introduction

For nearly five years, I have arrived at Touchstone's front door almost every Monday afternoon at 3:00 with a briefcase full of poetry books and a folder of typed poems from our creative writing session of the week before. When I come in, the girls gather excitedly around me wanting to speak of their lives –"Sharon, I had a good pass! Sharon, it's my birthday next week! Sharon, my cousin got shot last Saturday." Let's write about it", I say, and we all settle in together to begin another few hours of writing, reading and listening to each other's stories.

It doesn't always go smoothly, however. Touchstone is a residential treatment facility for female juvenile offenders in Litchfield, Connecticut. Almost all the girls have been involved with drugs, truancy, violence of all kinds, rape, abuse and running away – and they are teenagers, living in community, with all the emotional liability that accompanies adolescence. Our group meetings are lively and sometimes heartbreaking. Most of the girls are 15, 16, and 17, and are at Touchstone for approximately nine months. For most of them it is another placement in a system they have been part of for several years. There is much group processing, drug rehabilitation, and therapy along with school and the responsibilities of community living. The creative writing sessions are a special part of the program for a self-selected group of girls who love to write.

I volunteered myself in the summer of 1999 and the program has since expanded to include appearances on local radio and television stations, annual public performances at Artwell(a space in Torrington, CT that has graciously hosted us five times now), an annual poetry festival featuring the girls reading together with local woman poets, and appearances in various schools. We had a 2001 winner in the prestigious Hill-Stead Museum's Sunken Garden summer Poetry Festival; she read along with the five other finalists, to a crowd of 1500 in Farmington, CT. And, after a triumphant reading in April 2003 at The Hotchkiss School in Lakeville, CT we have continued to meet with a group of young women there for dinner and writing once a month, forming a most unlikely and amazingly successful small community of great emotional resonance.

But mostly, we just write. In response to my prompts of poetry, pictures, objects, or words as simple as "I remember" or "I'm afraid of", the girls tell their powerful stories, scribbling fast on torn-out pieces of notebook paper, which I take home and type up for them. I have files full of their work, and have long wanted to publish a chapbook, as I tell the girls over and over, "The world needs to hear your voices." And now, after 618 copies of the first edition of this chapbook have been sold and otherwise disseminated all over the world, I have realized a part of this dream and offer a much-expanded second edition with many more of their voices.

I believe adults are largely afraid of adolescents – there is a chasm between the generations that has been hard for both to bridge. Writing can do it. These poems can do it, have done it. I have seen awe and tears on the faces of our mostly adult audiences. My girls have transformed their short lives into art; their authenticity, the freshness of their expression, the insight into their experiences creates poems and stories that open our hearts, help us to understand why they are "locked up' in ways that studies and scholarly articles never can. There is nothing tentative about the way they express themselves. And writing is therapeutic too, often more than traditional therapy – the girls often say they write of things in creative writing that they do not speak of elsewhere. In our group, though the membership changes often because of all the comings and goings, confidentiality is highly valued and honored as the words are risked.

So much talent! I have culled from the work of nearly five years and many girls of diverse ethnicity and life experience – Puerto Rican, Latino, African American, Caucasian and combinations of all of these – a group of poems that represent many of the themes we touch on repeatedly. You will read of feelings about mothers and fathers, loss of virginity, violence, fear, rape and incest, loneliness, and proud self-description. You will read of who these young women truly are, underneath the label "juvenile delinquent", gang member, drug user or dealer, runaway. And, hopefully, you will think long and hard about what they face as they return to the world, you will look differently at young offender adolescents, you will wonder how you can help.

This book is a beginning – a beginning I think, of the possibility for understanding and compassion between races, generations, between those who are "different" from each other – a beginning sorely needed in today's torn-apart world. I hope it will offer you a glimmer of the hope, the empathy, the excitement and the learning that I have experienced each week as I write with the young women of Touchstone.

The world is made up of stories, not atoms.
– Muriel Rukeyser

Contents

Who I Am

The Real World

Running Away

A Poem Is a Chapter of Wisdom

a poem is a chapter of wisdom
words in your soul
they come naturally
as you flow
like a flower,
a poem just grows
on its own
when I write poems I flow
maybe not in a gangsta way
but in a thought out, well written way
a flower can tell its own story
or a chapter of a story
a book full of poems
can tell a story too
but poems aren't always so easy to write
my mind can go blank at any time
I can't say the things from my heart
I write down things that don't make sense
but then again, maybe they do
maybe that's what's really a poem
a real natural poem
what's inside my soul
there's my story of a real poem
a flower always grows
then it will die
my poem can burn
or be published for life

Y.R.

Why Am I Here?

Why am I here?
To get abused,
beat on,
cursed out?
Am I here to fight?
Argue?
Explain myself to people?
Do I have to go on living my life
the way I've been living it
or the way I'm living?
Maybe if I had been born white
my life would be a little better –
maybe a lot better.

Why am I here?
If I wasn't born
life for my parents would be better
(one less child to care for or worry about).

Why am I here?
I feel loved, but I don't.
Should I be here
or should I not?
If I was gone what would my family think?

I feel nothing at all –
or should I say only
my brothers and sisters would care
because they may know a little
of how I feel.

Really, no one knows how I feel.
No one.
There is not one person who can say
they actually know where I'm coming from
because no one does.
Some people say they do but I tell them,
You don't.

Why am I here?
Am I here to fall?
Am I here to stand?
Am I here to die
or am I here to live?

I don't think I need to be here.
I'm not wanted anywhere.

People say they love me
but I feel it's a lie.

I once said, *I love you*
to great grandma
but then she died.

This world is confused
and so am I.

Why am I here?
To live or to die?

S.K.

Do I Have To?

do I have to go through this pain?
do I have to wonder why
nothing's ever going to be the same?
or wonder if my dad loves me
or if he just doesn't give a damn?
do I have to live in this cold world
surrounded by drugs, guns and thugs
that sell me into the game?
do I have to feel the tears falling down my cheeks
because of this nigga?
do I have to see my mom struggle
while I sit here acting like I don't care?
what will it take for everything to be the same?
what will it take for people to realize youth is the future?

S.B.

When I Was Happy

long ago I was happy
when I had friends
not foes
when it was just me
my mom and sister
and no man
telling us what to do
I was happy
when I could be with my family
not his
I was happy
when I enjoyed being a child
instead of a woman
when I was restless
and wouldn't break down

those were good days
bitches weren't grimy
and didn't care about
who you be with
and what you do
I was happy
before my mother got married
before I started getting beat
for every little thing
before me and my sister
cried ourselves to sleep
every night
these days I'm not too happy
but I am glad
that my mom survived
all her struggles and sadness
I'm happy that she's divorced
and does what she wants

I'm happy because
me, my sister and my mom
are once again
on our own and alive
because we've made it
through the strife

L.W.

What I Miss

I miss being a child.
I can honestly say I was happy then.
Pictures of me then make me cry.
I couldn't stop smiling –
running around, falling down –
getting back up –
my mother so happy to see me.
It's like watching a movie of someone else's life.

I miss something
I never even knew.

B.H.

How It Started

Loneliness Go Away

Sometimes the feeling of being alone
takes over
loneliness haunts me, acts as
the beholder
traps my heart and frees my mind
pulling people away
from being loving and kind
I long to have the feeling
of being one of the crowd
eliminate dark rooms
with no one around
I suspect I'm the victim
of being lost in this world
no words to say
no smile to grin
loneliness again
the parting and separation
of heartbreaks and sorrow
loneliness has no name
nowhere to go
I trusted the happiness
that stayed with me for so long
now as it turns away
I'm thinking it did me wrong
shedding tears of anger
of loneliness at you in attack
happiness come back
happiness come back

C.H.

Something You Won't Forget

it all started when I was born
my mother was fourteen
she was on crack
yeah
my mother didn't want me
my dad was young
born into a bugged-out family
eighteen months in the hospital
because I was addicted to my mother's addiction
at three my mother left me alone
with my little ten month old brother
by the age of seven I started living with my father
by nine I had seen my Uncle Queenie hang himself
die and get cut down by the cops
at ten I started repping a gang
seen my stepmother stab my stepsister with a shank
by eleven years old I was molested
at thirteen I started stealing cars
fighting girls   smoking dust
drinking   popping
selling drugs   robbing people
repping my colors
strong
running away from cops
I've seen many people get shot in cold blooded murders
yet day by day
all I wanted was a hug
so I could cry
I've been abused, stabbed, cut and held at gunpoint
I remember when I just turned thirteen
I was so drunk
I decided to jump off the Stratford Bridge
I don't know who the man was
but he stopped me
I don't know why
but that made me really think about my life

that's when I turned myself in
and my brother Danny got shot
and then I realized I need to care about everything that I've done
    wrong
and how my life is
I must cherish my life
because myself is all I've got

I have no regrets

L.J.-L.

When I Was Thirteen

When I was thirteen
I always stayed out late –
you know the deal.
Yeah, I chillin'
with a lot of older people –
just did my own thing.
I did what I wanted to
and never cared
about who, what, where and why –
I needed the smoke.
I needed the drinks
to ease my mind
when I felt like too much was going on.
That's what led me to this place.

And I always heard a woman's voice saying
Oh wake up now
'cause it's only a dream.

A.O.

The First Time I Tried to Commit Suicide

The first time I tried
to commit suicide
I was angry
very saddened
depressed
very pissed off
I remember
I would always try
to cut myself
choke myself with a scarf
when I thought no one cared
I would swallow plastic
trying to choke
drink anything
that had to do with alcohol
that was the first time
I remember
when I cut up my leg
blood dripping everywhere
I remember
sniffing my meds
to pass out
or get sick

what happened?
maybe it was not my time to die
God did not want me to go
God saved me
He blessed me
because I know
the people who care about me
would miss me
I am so confused
but thanking God
for standing by my side

B.S.

Do You Know My Pain?

if you don't know me, why assume you do?
do you know my pain?
know how it feels?
how it shatters my whole life?
my pain
the pain of neglect and abuse by a mother
is disgusting
a selfish bitch who just isn't a person
but still she is my mother
that's my pain
my pain is my family
sexually abusing me
drugs and violence
saying it's all ok to do
saying *go ahead, love it*
that's my pain
I'm stuck with the evil life
family always says *never trust friends*
alone is pain
my pain is rape
do you know how it feels?
do you know how it fucking feels?
an innocent young body
still growing her capacity for love and care
being controlled by an evil being
an asshole with no heart or sympathy
do you know how it feels
having your ankles and wrists pinned to the floor
hearing your bones clicking
your inner thighs pressed to the ground
your lungs squeezed grasping for the air to scream?
with this burning flesh on you
you try
you try to fight, scream, defend your temple
you're just a little girl
he's grabbing his dick

forcing it into your body
my pain
conto cabron
furiously I try to close my legs
I'm scratching, pinching
still, everything rips to shreds
your life, your flesh
blood running down my cheeks

my family always says *never trust friends*
just because I was in pain from the ripping
and bleeding inside and out
my pain was this man
this evil man was family
how could he just ruin my dreams
my young life?

I'm waiting for the door to open
to learn there really is love and trust
to learn how it feels
my pain
my pain
I can't trust or love anyone else
I go my own way in life

I love you *abuelita*

N.V.

Never Told Until Today

1.

One day I stayed the night at my little sister's house –
we fell asleep on the couch with the music still playin'.

2.

I felt something on me so I woke up – her uncle
was on top of me with his pants down, holding
my mouth shut. I'm screaming but my sister
would not get up.

3.

He gets off me and I wake up my sister right next to me.
I told her what happened. She didn't believe me 'cause
the house doors were all locked. We woke up her mom
and her step dad and they searched the house. We all
fell back to sleep.

4.

It happens again; I feel something on me – it's him
but this time his pants are down and so are mine. He
tries to put it in but I kick him in the nuts. I scream
as loud as I can.

5.

My sister wakes up, so do her mom and step dad.
They call the cops and take him to jail.

6.

I never spend the night over there again,
even though he was locked up.

7.

A few months later we find out he's been doing this
to his own daughter since she was twelve years old.
Now she's seventeen.

I never told until today.

S.R.

The Most Horrible Day of My Life

I remember when my uncle used to beat on me –
when I was just a kid, he would drag me and kick me
with his size 12 or size 14 kind of black-ashy
working boots that look like they're from the army.
I remember when I ignored him or said how I feel
he ran up to me when I was warming hot water for my bath
and was going on to chill, he came into the bathroom
and pushed me and punched me in the back
and threw me in the steaming water –
I was getting treated like a rag doll.
I remember going to school with marks and crying
and not responding and scared to tell what was happening.
I remember when my uncle put a blade up to me
and said he was going to kill me, and saying that
he would sell me to his boys.
I remember when he abused me right in front of my mom
and I can see the fear and the sadness in her eyes
and there was nothing she could do but call 911.
I am lucky it wasn't too late.
I remember when my uncle put bleach in my cousin's shampoo
to be mean to her. Next I remember having a nice relationship
with this dude for two weeks and he has raped me.
I remember him hitting me and all the blood that came with that.
I remember getting slapped in the face by him, trying to hit him,
but it did not work. I remember going to the hospital
with a busted lip and bloody hands like I was not worth anything.
I remember going to detention and people were asking me what
    happened
and I just had nothing to say, just busting out with tears
and could not speak.

B.S.

It Breathes

my depression lives in me
was born in me
was raised in my soul
the feeling of the pain inside me
breaks me into pieces
I can feel it slice by slice,
all over my heart, mind,
and stomach
it lives in my stomach
it turns my stomach
and flips it, stirs it up
till my stomach gets upset
I lose my appetite
my desire for taste
my love for food
just disappears
depression takes over
its smell is strong, unbearable--
the smell of mold and sewer
it is the point where
depression has taken over my body
has me stuck in bed for weeks
the everyday smell
when the nightmare
is just sleeping
burnt rubber and smell of dirt
at the same time
its taste is like rotten things
just dumping up waiting
to be swallowed or spat out
a taste of death and glue
put together
its touch and feelings
affect my own
its power takes mine over
it's not a dream

it's reality
it has its own mind
its own soul
it's every woman's true nightmare
it's the depression
that lives
in me

N. V.

Warning

what can I say?
how can I let you know my struggles
express everything you need to know?
I can't
I can only let you know by my actions
my warning signs
I held up a red flag
no one acknowledged it
so I said whatever I wanted
did whatever I wanted
went to clubs
danced
drank
had the time of my life
but all that shit went by quick
got old fast
the dudes came and went
and yeah, they all had things to offer
but it didn't interest me
I needed a thrill
I got that thrill from doing illegal things
now I get my thrill from doing the right things
being a good person
but please
next time
pay attention to my red flags
before it is too late

L.V.

Puzzle Piece

locked in the basement
I guess that was sex time
for my mother and ex-stepfather
we cried
because we got bored
it was time to come back upstairs
I watch my mother get beat
I watch myself get beat
little then
I even thought of killing him
he broke my arm
just from hitting me one day
I remember it like it was yesterday
we wait outside
while my mother shops for food
I don't know exactly what I did
but when my mother got back
she didn't know what to do
she was young
married to an older man
there wasn't much that she could do
I went to the hospital
my mother and ex-stepfather
told the doctor I fell
or something
I just found out what my mother said
a year ago
I began to run with my mother
because we were the only ones he beat
I guess it was because I wasn't his child
now I wonder if this has an effect
on my life today
this puzzle piece
probably answers a lot
of questions

B.H.

24

Autobiography

I was kidnapped at six months.
What was my father's problem?

At five years old I was left all alone
watching my sisters while my mom wasn't home.

At six years old I had to move to Florida
due to drugs in my family.

For seven years I lived there – no contact
with my mom, with my sisters.
Not even with God.

At age twelve I moved back to Connecticut
where I belonged, but it was only one year
before I tried to end it all. I was in a hospital
for years because my life was too hard

At fourteen I got locked up for not going to school –
in a program with bitch ass fake rules. I ran
three times and got caught only once. I turned
myself in, instead of making a fuss.

My little sister got taken away, following
in the pattern I feel I have caused. She
doesn't go to school. I really don't know
why. Now she's in a hospital at twelve years old,
dying from a broken heart.

I'm fifteen years old. Where did my life go?
Can someone please tell me so I can find
my long lost way home?

H.J.

Abandonment

abandoned once again by the people
who supposedly care
they tell me *I'll be by your side*
but go on vacation
disappear
the people I look up to
seem so far away
I can never reach out my hand
because they are gone
it's so hard for me to settle down
I can't speak
I can't spread myself out
the voices I hear
are the guilt that I feel
maybe they left because I was there
it's too funny
how support can be so hurtful at times
one minute you speak
the next you're blind
you can never get close 'cuz
people won't always stay
whether they leave
or whether it's their day
to go to the great place
people have many reasons
for leaving your side
but can't explain why
they didn't say goodbye
yeah
it's hard to even hear these words
that make you feel like you got left alone
in this big world
I've felt abandoned so many times
that's why I'm strong now
– for living through all that pain

Y.R.

True Pain

I've been through lots of shit in my life.
gangs, drugs, guys, gurls, jail –
but something like this comes by
and tears me apart. I see him
when lil' things remind me of him –
or when I smell CK1 and Marlboros.
He'd smack me around when I tried to get up –
I'd struggle to stop him but he kept tearin' my shit up,
he hurt me, he made me cry. I wasn't a virgin,
I bled anyway. I finally got too tired to move,
but he kept going. When he was done,
he got drunk, then ten minutes later,
kicked my ass because I bled too much
on his bed. I cried the whole way home.

J.P.

Smooth Pain

my pain you can't touch
it's untouchable
even I can't touch it
I can only feel it
it's a smooth feeling
smoother than a baby's ass
smoother than teddy pendergrass
yes, but pain
pain when I walk
pain when I move
just smooth pain
sometimes people say
pain will heal
mine hasn't yet
it feels like the pain
my ancestors went through
it feels like the pain of a starving child
in the middle of the street
the pain of an old man robbed
of everything even his socks
the pain of the world
more pain
less pain
smooth pain

T.D.

Deep Dark Hole

ever since I was born
I've been torn
my crazy coke head father
stabbed my mother
tried to kidnap me
hit my grandma in the head
with a hammer
by the time I was three
that man was long gone

five years old
I got molested by my cousin
I won't forget that shit

the messed up thing was
my mom found out
and did nothing about it

always with mom and sis
till mom got her wish –
she got married when I was seven
I was so jealous and confused

everything was all good that first year
then all hell broke loose
that man had me and my sister
in his screwed-up rules
he hated me
because I was a momma's girl

I felt like I was in a cage
couldn't be alone with my mom no more
anything I did
he beat the shit out of me

I was too scared to go home after school
especially if I got a bad grade
or had done something wrong

I hate that man
he's one of the reasons
I got in so much trouble

'cause after three years I said
I've had enough of him
went out every day
came home when I wanted to
started getting real mean to people
and knocking bitches out
'cause they had a lot of mouth

started doing drugs
skipping school
getting arrested
not caring where I rested my head

one day my stepfather made me flip
I threw a big-ass knife at him
that's when he finally left me alone

I felt free at last

L.W.

Alone

I don't want to admit it
it was easier to lie
hold all the hurt and emptiness
smile instead of cry
I didn't want to face the fact
my life is full of pain
I long to stop my bleeding heart
and maybe smile again
I feel so forgotten
so betrayed
so alone
without a trace of forgiveness
and no soul to call my own
I didn't want to admit the fact
my wishes have no home
I'll return to anguish –
bow my head and cry alone

D.R.D.

The Best Gift

The best gift I ever got was the gold chain
with the praying hands –
a cross and a diamond on the hands.
My mom gave it to me.
Ooh child I was souped!
I rocked it for like a year.
It broke while I was dancing.
then my uncle stole it.

Second best – my gold XX's and OO's ankle bracelet
that my grandma gave me for Valentine's Day.
It was so cute
but I broke it.

Third best – the gold earrings my mom bought me.
They were nice too.
I lost one of them outside of dancing school.

Fourth gift – my two carat diamond earrings.
Damn, they were hot,
and they were real.
I let a boy I liked named Ernest wear them.
Then I got kicked out of school.

My X and O chain with the matching bracelet –
I still have that now.
They are not broken, knock on wood.
No but wait – I broke the clasp on the bracelet in my sleep.

But the most sentimental gift
was the ring my grandma gave me.
She used to let me sport all her rings.
I was ten and I threw it in a field.
Then I went to go look for it and it was gone.
I couldn't find it.

See, I've lost all my most prized jewels.
Ma, stop wasting your money!

J.H.

Red Light

stop everything

beauty
sex
money
cars
diamonds
jewelry
music
power

do these things equal love?
and if you have them
please give me some
because
I have none
of the above

L.V.

Where I Come From

Where I Come From

where I come from
fathers don't come back
where I come from
people die every day
where I come from
little girls always get raped
where I come from
you hear gunshots every hour
where I come from
people die in front of your face
where I come from
newborns are HIV positive
where I come from
teenage boys and girls are smoking crack
where I come from
little girls sell their bodies
where I come from
that's where I come from

S.R.

In My World

in my world
people die on the street
sell drugs to people
to make money for their kids and families
steal cars to go places
and shoot up their space
they pawn their mother's jewelry
and blame it on the kids
in my world
life's a bitch
I can't even buy me a fifty cent soda
without getting stripped
raped and hurt
babies and more
complications
no remorse
trouble in school
trouble on the street
that's why I'm in a facility
moms aren't there
fathers disappear
I hear this bullshit
that he does crack
can't get on the right track
well what about me
and all my needs
my hurt, my tears?
people who left me?
what about my world?
I can't enjoy it
I lived it
fucked it
made sure I had fun
in my world
I played some cards
that tell me my future

and when I saw my life
it was full of confusion
manipulations and more

that's what's inside
my world

Y.R.

My Streets

my block is too hot
too hot for my own damn good
but I mean what do you expect
I'm livin' in da fuckin' hood
the drug dealers, oh god
what can I say about them
all 1 know is they all over
straight down to the bums
and the drugs, same thing –
everybody want some
if it looks and smells good
niggas buying it
no matter where it come from
disease, that's another
almost every bitch in da beat got some
but they don't give a damn –
they shag the next nigga
now he scared to tell his niggas he's burning
shit's tough but its only the beginning
everyday it's like I'm at a funeral
instead of a wedding
yeah dem little boys they out
getting bitches pregnant and shit
but when the baby comes
none of them wants to baby sit
then we got the hoes
I just want to spit in they face
they only fuckin' up the creation
of the black girl's race
it's ridiculous –
our women brainwashed so bad
he done took my car to get some bitch
now I gotta catch a cab
in da hood we got young girls out having seeds
I've tried to help them
but they asses just don't listen

that's why half their babies diseased
the streets so grimy it's only unexplainable
if you smart enough you know
it's like a game at the spades table
but beware of the crackheads stealing anything
to sell to get by
some family members (the gangsta ones)
sit on the porch for them
like dumb asses to walk by
if you ask me
how anyone can survive the streets
hell I wouldn't know
I guess you gotta be a playa like me
and as long as I got my niggas
watchin' my back
ain't no way them monsta niggas
got nothing on what we stack
but the streets too thorough
if you ain't from the hood
'cuz when them friends see you comin'
they runnin' after what's good

these are my streets

S.K.

The Heart Beat

the heartbeat is crazy
that's where I'm from
the drugs, the money, the sex
the niggas, the bitches and the jumps
the nicks, the dimes –
I could go on forever
pagers everywhere
they just want to get high
girls talking shit
always wanting to fight
and the niggas – they real
but they ain't no good
a lot of them burning
on the block –
the Deuce, Garden, Vine,
Wes, the field
I bet not one bitch come in my block
poppin' that shit
niggas don't care –
they'd shoot anyone
for talking that dumb stuff

the buses
don't let me forget about them
everybody always needs a dollar
so they can take their broke ass home
the police
or the "boys"
is what I call them
they stay baggin' niggas
right in they box
cash and smoke stay swallowing
everybody think they grown

my hood is real –
just like a little New York
only reason people go to school
is to see their friends
the fights man – they ain't no joke
and unless your people is real people
they'll stand there and let your brains
get stomped out.
so that's the nigga where I come from
the Flamingo Hotel is where all the jumps go

you see
there's nothing good about where I come from
we got our own talk
our own walk
everybody the same
the streets suck you in
my brother always says –
today may be my last day

S.B.

My Kitchen Table

my kitchen table is the hangout
we don't eat there but we express ourselves there
how many kids does so and so have?
how many times have the bill collectors called?
how much is the phone bill?
that's the food on my kitchen table
we eat the gossip in the air
we eat our wisdom at the kitchen table
not the wisdom of books and school
but the wisdom of the projects,
welfare dick, fast cars, drug money –
our kitchen table is as well-rounded
as if the Mafia were there
fuck my kitchen table
there's nothing there to eat
I've been eating the same shit there forever
I want different foods at my kitchen table
no gossip or shit from the streets
I want the food of books and school
how to make it
I want to digest the food at my kitchen table
let it move through my system
return again at the table
fuck the food at the projects, welfare dick,
fast cars and drug money
I want some new food at my kitchen table

T.D.

Schooling

Young kids dying
from suburban malaria –
what happened to the goodness
of going to school at seven
with a *Barney* lunch box?
They will never see that day.
What's going on?
Junior high, violent words spit
at you with gnawing teeth
of words like kick rocks –
what do you do?
Teachers that talk about
how they think your parents,
your house, have such a stench
that *Febreeze* can't take it out.
Is that wrong?
High school –
your heart is beating
like the nuclear bombs
in the world wars
that kill you from the inside.
Mother can't help you now
they say with a disappointing
grin – parties that influence your brain
as if you were a vegetable
without salt and pepper –
you deadly chef.
College – what do you want to do
with no future ahead of you?
Deadly lines telling you
you're not going to make it.
Graduation – drinking 100 proof –
not giving a damn.
You're old now
smoking shit laced
with god knows what –

stressful days in school
your whole life.
You're killing yourself
slowly.
What's next? you ask
Dead?
Alive?

T.D.

I'm Afraid Of

I'm afraid of that tall dark man
with the deep ass voice
you know
when I was walking home
the one that dragged me
into the backseat of his car
the one that touched me
in unwanted places
at unwanted times
the one that stuck his penis
in between my beautiful thick thighs
I'm afraid of that man
that caused me pain today
the one that ruined my life
and caused me to run away
I'm afraid of that man
I don't know who he is
I think if I were ever to see him again
I would recognize who he is

S.C.

Robbery

you took it
the most valuable thing I had
why?
why did you choose to ruin my life?
did you think you were right to take it
without permission?
what makes you think it was okay to hurt me?
did someone lie to you?
I wish I could say it was a good day for me
it wasn't
it was wrong
you took my innocence
my life
all the other things I should have loved at ten
you asshole
you took my virginity by force
for that I hate you
you took it like a thief in the night
the most valuable thing I had

S.O.

The Night She Would Never Forget

dedicated to all girls who have experienced incest

as she lays quietly
on her bed
the door opens slowly
the sounds on the steps wake her
who is there
Don't be afraid
he replies
as she goes back to her sleep
he grabs her
her mouth is covered
the house is empty
the horror begins
when she felt the pain and hate
and everything
suddenly stops
she sits in her bed
covers covering
her entire body
she's bleeding to death
she's crying her heart out
she can't imagine
why the only person she had
could hurt her
in such a way
she says to herself
Why, Daddy?

R.O.

Why Is It That?

why is it that
where I come from
it seems like the world
is never gonna change
I wake up to watch the weather
and see the face
of another young person
who got shot
nothing ever changes for the better
where I come from
it changes for the worst
why is it that
where I'm from
older guys always want to rape little girls
get them pregnant
but never want to stick around
take responsibility for what they did
where I'm from
I hope a change comes
because one is definitely needed

S.C.

Who I Am

Wanna Be Me

walk in my shoes
hurt your feet
then you'll know
why I do dirt in the streets
you walk around
try to look down on me
cause you can't be me
you whisper in corners
call out my name
but have you walked in my shoes?
have you hurt your feet?
then, no, you don't know why
I do dirt in the streets
who told you you could talk shit about me?
who told you it was ok to plot on me?
was it my gear, my chains, earrings, bracelet?
all you do is hate
do you wanna be me?
if you do then walk in my shoes
hurt your feet
and then you'll know why
I do dirt in the streets

S.O.

How I Feel Deep Inside

A smile is what I show
a happy teen is what they see
not knowing what's running through my mind
my name is hidden behind my smile
not the name I am called by
but the name of despair and care
I have black hair
fair skin
a bright face
very slim
very attractive
hazel eyes
a cute style
I say and tell and talk
with lies about life
how it really is trife
I speak words of joy
they're flavored with sugar and spice
but I am a lonely person
a depressed child
a hopeless being
I dream and wonder
of all the things I want
to have and be
I have it all in material and gold
but not in comfort and care
life is all sugar coated
sweet as candy
creamy as caramel
rich as chocolate
life is what you make it
but I had no choice
I was born, raised and beaten
now I live

speak at the age of sixteen
feeling helpless with the letters I'm called by
like there's a big world around me
and I'm just here created
by a higher power
I feel shame and guilt
for things I never caused
I feel the pain in my body
for another person's falls
I cry for the sadnesses of this world
that are not being seen
but a smile is what I show
a tear is never seen
I suffer in my heart
from this cruelty around me
I have fallen into the spell
of this world
I will not continue
with the false sweetness
of this life beside me
I will break these chains
express how I feel
be called by my real name
that I will truly reveal

N. V.

A Piece of String

I am like a piece of string
I am sturdy
I am slender
I can be tough
and I can be tender
pull on me
I get real tight
try to cut me
I put up a fight
if you're nice
I'll do things right
if you're gentle
I'll come apart

when your heart tears at the seams
I'll sew its pieces together

D.D.

The Blurred Vision My Shades Bring

my vision is blurred
why? I don't know
but wait – I do
I have forced myself to wear shades
they are thick, hard to see through
like a tinted window
it's not that I don't see well
it's just that I'm not used to seeing
myself led the right way
my thick glasses have been self-inflicted
I'm so used to being on the run
not listening to anyone
that little by little, my thick shades
have been shaped to the exact form of my face
a cop-out, they are my way of looking at other people
not taking the chance of them knowing that I'm seeing them
it's my way of staying within myself
my glasses don't let me see the sun
they don't let me see anyone's true colors
I see black and white, I don't see grey
with my glasses, there is no *anything is possible if you try*
until the day I take down my protective shades
I will never see myself or any other people
loved for who they truly are

so today I decide to take them off!

D.D.

Journeys

Am I there yet?
I ask myself often
where did I begin?
I've lost track.
I chose a path that was dark and cold
but I wasn't alone.
That's what made it easy –
I had a hand to hold.
Now I feel like I'm at a rest stop
with a thousand different directions to go in.
The one I'm turning to is the one that I know.
I've gone this way more than once
and really don't have much to show.
I've considered a new direction –
even gone a few miles in
wondering if that old path
was just somewhere to begin.
I know I've got it in me
but I question if it's a good lead.

Sometimes what you want can hurt you
and life is under no obligation
to give us what we need.

J.I.

I'm Scared

I am scared of life and how the outcome of everything
will affect my future.
I'm scared to face my siblings, father, let alone
my own cousin.
I'm scared of who I will hurt
if I make the wrong decision.
I am scared of walking the streets
all alone at night.
I am scared to look at myself emotionally,
verbally and physically.
I am scared that I will not make it,
so why bother to try?
I'm scared of getting too close to people
because I have to say goodbye.
Where is the good in good-bye?
Because I cry at the thought of loneliness.
I'm scared to live my life
but I'm even more scared to end it
because I know it will give pain to my family.
I'm scared to reveal myself
because I'm afraid of rejection.
I'm scared of how my siblings view me –
But, most of all, I think
I'm scared of myself.

M.K.

I'm Dying Inside

I'm dying inside
because I have no self-respect.
I'm dying inside
because for the past eleven years
I couldn't control my life.
I'm dying inside
because I'm scared of life.
I'm dying inside
because of the way I present myself on the outside.
I'm dying inside
because I'm feeling so lonely.
I'm dying inside
because I have no one to hold me.
I'm dying inside
because my home is not safe.
I'm dying inside
because my life is fake.
I'm dying inside
because I can't let go of the fact that I was raped.
I'm dying inside
because I've built so much hate.
I'm dying inside
because I'm so confused.
I'm dying inside
because I was manipulated, mistreated and used.
I'm dying inside
because I hate myself.
I'm dying inside
because I'm hurting others.
I'm dying inside
because I never had a childhood.
I'm dying inside
because I need a dad.
I'm dying inside
because I am consistently sad.

I'm dying inside
because I have so much anger.
I'm dying inside
because I'm slowly committing suicide.

M.K.

That Time In My Life

that time in my life
when I felt so alone
that time in my life
when I wondered
how it would feel
to never have been born
I've been through so much
I'm scared forever
why did God put me through
such bad weather?
I wanted to choke myself
because I felt I was such a failure
people don't understand
a word can ruin a person forever
that's why you should always think
before you speak
because you could be the reason
a person ends up in a box
yes
I can admit
I tried to kill myself before
but I couldn't see myself
falling to the floor
I'd rather cry than die
because there's always a better day
no matter what comes my way

S.B.

The Real World

The Real World

the real world
that we're hidin' from
(the one we're supposed to be
protected from)
from what reality?
they fail to understand
life demands and expands
that's the plan

the violence is the silence
of people who confess
protest
and could care less
about community
or unity
world wide
homicide
suicide

you sell crack
probation, community service
to give back
what type of shit is that

the real world is a screwed up place
so try to keep up to its pace
or reality will slap you in the face

for sex you flex
get in line
next
are put through a test

reality leads to fatality

A.L.

Drugs

they ruined my life
my mother did them
for almost all her life
they messed our family up
for parents chose drugs over us kids
then I started to use
and they all put up a fuss
my father's still addicted
thank god, my mother stopped
I used to put the pain on them
that one day made me drop
something that no one knows –
I was young when I picked up
my first blunt, my first forty

I was real young
I tell everyone eleven and twelve
not even my family really knows
I was eight
in my school's P.E. room

at nine I got introduced
to booze
my father used to let me get drunk
he really didn't give a damn
but now I've stopped
I've seen what it's done
but oh no
I still need to run
they still live with me
in more than one way
no one will ever know
why I need to run

it's the drugs

H.J.

He Raped Me

he touched me and kissed me
without my permission
he slapped me and bruised me
I kicked him in his shins
he pushed me and fought me
threw me on the floor
I jumped up
grabbed his head
lashed it through the door
we fought and kicked
yanked and yelled
he told me to be quiet
because no one was gonna tell
I told him *hell no*
spit in his face
than I ran like hell at a flock of birds pace
he chased me
caught me at the bottom of the stairs
that nigga pulled me by my head
snatched out all my hairs
I swung me arms oh so hard
hit him in the lips
they bled real bad
I turned and grabbed him
by his ass tips
he grabbed me by my neck
then reached for a plastic bag
I foamed at the mouth
choked and barely gagged
I managed to loosen
his so-tight grip
he slid on a shirt
turned around then slipped
he grabbed me and some string
tied me to the bed
then got up and said

you 'bout to give me some head
I cried and cried
but he didn't stop
he pulled down his pants
forced it in
something popped
I prayed and prayed
for him to stop
dear lord
he took something away from me
which I truly adored
I'm sad and wished
that he wouldn't have taken it away
for when God comes down to judge him
he must right then and there pay
a man took something special
made it hard for me to be me
I told him no
he took it anyway
that man, he fucking raped me!

S.K.

Gang Life

Black men, black boys, black girls
babies, adults, everyone – gang related.
Nowadays, if we look at gang life around my way
it's mostly babies, the majority black.
So much of our society is made up of gangs.
And the majority of gangs are made up of our black men –
or, shall I say, our young black men.
The boys of the gangs aren't the trouble –
maybe it's the streets themselves?
But it can't be the streets – or could it?
The streets and gangs around my way suck you in quick –
you don't have time to say no to them.
They are too many. And knowing our men
like they are falling. They kill and fight
the ones that should be protected.
They give little ones the guns to watch out
when they should be somewhere playing.
It's tough – the gang life isn't what I would call life.
Most of our black men are lucky to be alive.
It's sad to say but this is no time to sit down and cry –
if your son was in a gang you would see for what people die.
I mean damn – it's gang life!

S.K.

Confused and Guilty

I have a lot of cousins on both my Mom's side and my Dad's.
I remember when I went shopping one day
I saw one of my cousins from my Mom's side –
he brought me home.

My cousins on both sides are in gangs.
So one day, my cousin on my Dad's side
wanted to set up one of my cousins from my Mom's side.
Half of them know they are both my cousins.
I didn't know what to do – I'm not tryin' to set up
one of my cousins for my other cousin.

I was so confused.
I didn't know what to do, didn't want to have
anyone in my family die –
I told my dad's nephew I wasn't gonna do it.
Then a couple of weeks later, I find out
the cousin who wanted me to set up my cousin
on my Mom's side – they both were found dead
at the basketball court at the park.
I thought I was doing the right thing
by saying no – now I feel like a guilty bitch.

S.R.

Lovely Drugs

another fear
another tear
another year

it seems like a life cycle
a cycle of depression
that leads into another cycle
a cycle of aggression

I take life in vain
I need to slow down
my heart is always left with pain
on my face a frown
why do I continue to hurt myself?
is the rush worth it?
can't I see it affects my health?
why couldn't I just quit?

now I'm stuck doing another year
shedding another tear
fighting another fear
the fear
of being lonely

D.R.D.

Saying No

Saying no to drugs is sometimes hard to do.
I do love not to feel or think about what's going on.
I do think first at times before I do it –
I say it really isn't worth it to get a dirty urine –
but then again I have that thought,
I don't want to feel,
so I just do it anyway.
Saying no to people is hard for me at times –
like when they ask to borrow something
because I'm just the kind of person who says
if you don't have none, the why not give you some?
Now, it's kind of different –
I'm trying to get to that point –
I have come to realize that people take advantage of me
when it comes down to these things,
so now I'm trying to start saying *no*.

No is a word I don't like to receive.
Saying no is also sometimes hard for me
because I think of the love I want that I'm not getting –
so I just say *Fuck it.*

Not saying *no* to someone or something from the beginning
is painful and regretful because you wish you could take
        everything back.
No is a two letter word –
I need to start using it more
to get where I want to get in life.

T.M.

The Day I Said Good-bye

I just sat there, staring at the casket through the sermon –
I don't think I even blinked.
I mean, my best friend killed himself –
now he's somewhere
lost in my cluttered mind.
The speech is over.
I walk to the open casket –
I look at him.
He doesn't look dead, maybe he's sleeping.
I touch his face and it's cold.
I realize he really is dead.
I stare.
Tears stream down my reddened cheeks.
No! No!
I'm screaming.
I grab hold of him –
Don't leave me! Don't go!
His mom and dad try to pry me away –
too weak with their loss.
I finally let go.
forever.

J.P.

The Real World

the truth is
that nobody
really gives a shit about you
if someone does
you're lucky
this is a cold world
you have to build yourself up
to be prepared to be
knocked down
to be left
sometimes
to even have to learn
on your own
it's sad
but that is life
the real world is what we live in
you can't walk it with closed eyes
it's true that sometimes
you can't even trust
your own blood
shit – it ain't right, your own kind
screwing you over
it's not a game
even though there are many similarities
but the difference is –
lives are being taken.

B.H.

I Lost My Heart

the day has come
when my heart would split
split into a direction
because of fuss
and miscommunication
my heart is always meant to love
it doesn't hate
let alone break up
what did I do
what could I say?
my heart went in one direction
not his
so now I realize my heart is gone
he doesn't have it
but someone else does
I just wish I knew
who had my lost heart
so I can get it back
work my shit out
learn to move on

I'm afraid
I'll never find
my lost heart

Y.R.

Night Thoughts

I stayed up real late last night
thinking of you.
Pulled the covers over my head
said I was through.
Am I ready to say *We can't*
and walk away?
Or do I need another day?
You fill a gap in my life
that I don't quite understand
You're the one who broke me,
you understand?
Who else will love me like you do?
Who else will know what it was like to steal?
Who else shares the passion for the things we feel?
What's brought us together
feels like it's torn us apart.
Where did we go wrong?
Why did we start?
We were perfect for each other
in all the wrong ways –
I did you wrong to keep my distance.
I showed you love to keep you near.
I told you forever
and forever is what I fear.

J.I.

The Real World

The real world is like hell.
Everyone has been there.
No one is perfect, no one
doesn't have anything
wrong with them.

The real world is sex,
drugs, violence and fun–
a forest of wild niggas looking
for a piece of raw meat
like a pack of wolves
or lions ready to attack –
a pool of nasty naked
chicks ready to open
up like clams, at any given
moment. I've been there,
done that.

The real world is just one
big test. If you pass, you
live. If you fail, you die.

J. W.

Running Away

Running Away

I'm the track star of this tournament
I've got the championship
I've won the gold
I know I can't stay still
running away is bold
I stop in my tracks
I sit still, don't move
running away – there's so much I could lose
my life, my problems, I'm inside in this game
competing is still in my way
the trophy they want – or my life –
I leave behind
work things out
I use my mind
I'm selfish, I've lost so much
but in the world around me
I want all the luck
running away
time is not on my side
I sit back and think
I could run forever
but can I really depend on my feet
to make my life better?
I'm the track star of this tournament
I've won the gold
now I can't stay still
running away is so bold
I run right through the wall of pain
continue to run that way
I get no where
I'm back where I started
shame and grief
running away – I can't live in peace
I need food to eat and a place to sleep
he tells me, *You're not gonna depend on me*
I get the fuck out, I'm right back on the streets

I tighten my shoelaces
because my life now depends on my feet

C.H.

A Runaway's Cries

I know it's true
what a fool, I've run away
for too long – my life is hard
but the streets are much harder
scared, hurt, lost, alone
my only cries
a runaway's cries
I missed my mom
I think of the love behind
the doors of my house
but a fear overcomes the joy
I'm afraid to enter my door
– no particular reason why
I am full of so much
to get it out would take years
and I still have my only cries
a runaway's cries

can you dry my tears?
stop my cries?
do you understand me
through my sobs
– if you asked how many times
I've run away
I would respond
enough
if you asked how many times
someone tried to soothe
my runaway tears
I would say
none
so I continue alone
with my lonely cries
a runaway's cries

S.O.

A Little Runaway

I am a little runaway
I always run   maybe
because my mom did
drugs   I did not know
how to deal with it
the only way I do
is to run   now I deal
with it by talking

D.C.

I've Run In Different Ways

I've run in different ways.
When I was sad or upset – you'll see
me running from my feelings.
When I was scared and afraid you'll see
me running from my fears.
When I was with my family and friends
you'll see me running from their love.
When I had no one to care and be by my side
you'll see me running from loneliness.
When someone was always right and I was wrong
you'll see me running from the truth.
When someone made fun of me you'll see
me running from embarrassment.
When the night turns pitch black you'll see
me running from the darkness.
When I was hurting inside you'll see
me running from my pain.
When trouble came knocking at my front door
you'll see me running through the back door.
When I start thinking and all of a sudden stop
you'll see me running from my thoughts.
When everyone is laughing and having fun
you'll see me running from excitement.
When I have a question you'll see me
running from the answers.
When tears run down my face you'll see me
running from my cries.
When I stand and look in the mirror you'll see me
running from my reflection.
When I stare and get amused you'll see me
running from my reactions.
When I walk down the street all alone you'll see
me running from my shadow.
And now I run to seek love – something I lost –
I run to seek care – something that was never there.

R.O.

Sitting Here

sitting here
playing spades
I hear my brain say
run away
as the world starts to fade
sometimes
I feel like turning away

run away
feeling like an underground slave
run away
that's all the blunt says

go, leave, run, leap
puff, puff
that's what the blunt says

run away
die
let the words fade away

leave me alone
I'm tryin' to play spades

L.J-L.

Parents

what mama said

mama said I was too young to bring you up
mama said I'm confused and totally abused
mama said I'm the mother, you're the child
mama said play the game – don't let the game play you
mama said men only want one thing
they steal, kill and deceive
so keep your legs closed
mama said trust no one
mama said I did the best I could
I never did nothin' wrong
it's your daddy's fault
mama said I'm surprised you're not pregnant
mama said I wish you were never born
ladies don't stay out late at night
pour me another glass of wine
damn that cut was so damn fine
mama said you make me sick
get me something to drink
walk the dog
take care of the baby
get an education
grow up to do what I never did
mama said I'm doin' my part you do yours
mama always said this, that and the third
but never understood one of my words

girls of creative writing, winter 2004

Mommy, Don't Leave

I was on my knees crying
tugging on your shirt
begging you please mommy
please don't leave
don't leave me alone
I need you mommy
please don't leave
good-bye baby, I love you
you said to me
as you walked
towards the flight attendant
I was lonely
with puffy eyes
a runny nose
crying
as I cry I say good-bye
mommy I love you
but inside I felt something
good-bye was different today
I was saying good-bye for a long time
and it made me cry even more

B.F.

Mother, Where Are You?

mom, I ask why sometimes,
why did you have to leave me?
I think sometimes I am lonely without
a mom to hold me in the darkness
bring me to light
mom, you're beautiful
number one
strong
confident
able
I cried your name on those days
that I didn't have you by my side
who are you?
I know you as crazy, mean, insecure, lonely
I want a mom
you're still there
but why don't I know who you are?
In the night I cry for you
wishing you could be the fairy godmother
that made all my dreams come true
the scent of your perfume
the smile on your face
the smooth texture of your skin
mommy believe me that I need you
there's a section in my heart that you belong in
life's not over yet for me to find you
you're somewhere, I know
yes, I live with you
you're the lady who screams, yells, swears
but maintains
mother, you're supposed to be everlasting in my life
I feel that you have just started
do you hate me?
do you still want to be my mommy?
do you love me to death?
I don't want to lose you

but first I have to find you
mother please never go
take time to get to know me for me
love me, hug me, laugh with me
I'm not afraid of you
but who are you?

C.H.

You Told Me

You told me you would always love me.
I'll always love you too.

You told me to be up by ten.
I'd wake up at noon.

You told me I could always talk to you.
I chose not to speak.

You told me to go to every class.
I only went to two.

You told me time was running out.
I laughed and looked at my watch.

You told me to be off the phone by nine pm –
the battery went dead.

You told me to quit smoking.
I opened both my windows instead.

You told me to call if I needed help.
I must have forgotten the number.

You told me I looked tired.
I yawned and said *So do you*.

You asked me where your money was.
I said I didn't know.

You asked me where I was going.
I just left and slammed the door.

J.I.

Losing a Bond

She was my best friend in the world.
I could tell her anything.
We trusted each other –
respected each other.
We went out together
and had fun.
We told jokes and laughed.
I took care of her
when she was sick.
She took care of me
when I was sick.
She was the shoulder I cried on
and she was the mother
who made me feel better.
Now all of that is gone
We no longer tell jokes and laugh.
We no longer trust and respect each other.
We just don't even bother with each other.
What happened?
Where did things go wrong?
Where's my mom?

L.B.

Mom

Can you help me?
Can you love me?
Can you play with me?
Can you talk to me?
Can you show me the right way?
Can you hold me?

D.C.

The Feelings

I had these feelings
that I needed to express to my mother.
I really did not have the guts to tell her,
but I did anyway.

I told her I felt lonely, not loved or cared about.
And that that's how I felt every day.
She was shocked to hear me say this
because she never would have thought
I felt this way.

She said she's sorry she made me feel this way;
she said she's always thinking of me
every time of the day.

She told me that she would do anything
to show me how much she loves and cares.
I told her to hush, just to hug me
like I was a teddy bear.

S.R.

The Unclaimed Daughter

I am different.
I am unique.
(You thought different).
I am who I am.
I like girls.
But you don't approve of this.
You are ashamed of me.
You said I wasn't your daughter.
I can't say it's not true.
I can't say I'm just playin'.
I am who I am.
And if you can't accept me
for who I am
I will remain unclaimed.

B.F.

Mommy, Why Don't You Love Me?

Mommy, why don't you love me?
I feel as though you don't love me –
as though you don't want me anymore.

I feel as if you've abandoned me –
thrown me away – given me up to the world.

Right now , at this moment,
I feel as though I shouldn't be here –
I'm not wanted.

I feel you put me here
so the world could walk all over me.

Mommy, why don't you love me?

I hate you
I hate you
I hate you

These are the words I say in my head
as I get beat up by strangers.

Help me, mommy! Help me!
are the words I scream.

My voice fades away –
my mind is wound up –
you are nowhere to be found.

I'm lying here just like a helpless pup.

I lie there waiting for you to come.
You don't turn up even in pity.
I think to myself, *You stupid scum.*

Mommy, why don't you love me?
I miss you so very much.
Mommy, why don't you love me?
I am way down in the dirt.

S.K.

I'm Sorry

mom, you're a pretty black queen
I know you wonder why I did those things I did
I didn't mean to hurt you
I'm just so confused
all I wanted to do
is what I wanted to do
I didn't care if I hurt you
don't think I wasn't listening
when you used to talk
it's just that we were both wrong
we both did something bad
ok – I know you're the mother and I'm the child
but your child is young in age
old in the mind
to you I'm your little girl
but if you look into his eyes
I'm a girl with hips and thighs
ass and pretty feet
he didn't care about my age
hell I didn't either
remember when I used to come home late
and you asked me where I was?
I said I was at my friend's house
well I was
I just wasn't with her
I was in his room
while he took over my body
I talked about him so much
I tried to give you a clue
I think you know

S.B.

What Mama Sees, What Mama Says

ten toes
ten fingers
two eyes
one nose
brown eyes
more precious than gold
I wish I could have seen this
sixteen years ago
I'm sorry for grandpa
he doesn't really hate you
he just thought having you
at age 14 was disgraceful

I am sorry that before your life began
mine was unmanageable
I am sorry that I cannot find it in me
to say *I love you*
I really think that my life
would've been better
if I had lost you
I know you've grown up to be
just like me
but please
never have heroin shots
running through your baby's IV
I know on April 10 I told you I'd be back –
turned around and shut the door
and that was the end of that

but listen to me, I am the mommy
no matter what
you are my baby and I'll always
come back for you.

L.J.-L.

To Dad

Dad, why did you leave?
If you didn't want me
why did you fuck my mother?
You left us both
and now I've grown up.
You take things as a joke.
You damn bastard –
I had nobody to turn to.
You didn't love me –
you abandoned me.
I needed you when mom wasn't there.
I needed you to tell me about boys.
I was young and stupid
to say, "Mom, he'll come back,"
but I was wrong and mom was right.
I hate you.
I wish you were dead.

C.S.

Locked Up

Things I Was Told Not To Do

In life I have been told
not to do many things
but I was rebellious
and decided to do them
anyway.
I got in a lot of trouble
but I didn't listen
and now I see better
than ever why
I've had some consequences
in my life.
I might not have learned
completely but I know not
to do those things.
If only I had listened
so long ago
my life
would have been
a piece of cake.
But I'm the type
who wants to see
things for herself
never wanting to take
others' learning experience.
My life could
have been easier if I did,
but I'm glad I didn't
because I wouldn't
have met the people I know
or the learned the things
I have learned.

J.S.

Just For Fun

hanging out with my friends
it was just for fun

skipping school
it was just for fun

smoking a little weed
it was just for fun

disrespecting my mother
it was just for fun

went on the run
it was just for fun

got arrested
it was just for fun

now look where I'm at
this shit ain't fun

L.B.

I Remember

I remember the first time I got locked up.
It was nothing.
I laughed about it, made jokes about it;
little did I know how scary it truly was.
I feel like after two years of being away from home
I need to gasp for air.
It doesn't come naturally.
Every day I'm hoping to get out of here,
even if it's for just an hour.
I remember the first time I got locked up
I went home four days later.
Now, it's going on two years and it's no joke.
I dread places like this even if I don't show it, I feel it.
Nothing can ease my pain, not even my mother.
I remember when I was free and happy
and now I'm drowning in misery ,
feeling weary, not knowing if I'm coming or going.
My head aches for love.
All I want is one more chance
to prove to everyone I can make it,
and I will, even if I need a push here or there.
My life feels like it is ending,
even though it's just beginning.
I feel old with pain, not wanting to see
the fame I once knew at home or in the streets.
The one thing I can remember is being free,
having the power to be me.

J.S.

First Night In Detention

it was the worst day of my life
I thought I was strong
guess I was wrong
I didn't know what to do
I didn't know anyone
I remember wishing I could take
everything I had done back
sitting on my bed all alone
was the worst kind of loneliness
I had ever felt
all the thoughts
that went through my mind
all the pain
regret
my freedom was taken from me
and that was the reality

L.B.

Change

being where I am has forced me to change
change my state of mind
change the way I approach situations
change my way of living

but where I am I'm still not free
I feel like a caged bird with clipped wings
unable to say what I please
unable to go where I want to
unable to be free

being in the system has taught me nothing
except how not to get caught the next time
how to get around the restrictions
how to get where you need to go by manipulating

being in the situation I'm in
I've had to learn how to advocate for myself
I've had to learn how to stand up
to the injustices that go on
I've learned to speak the truth
because to them
the truth is unjust

if you're in the system long enough
you start to wonder why you can't say certain things
you start to wonder why things get covered up
you start to wonder why the system is just corrupt

first impressions are lasting
my impression of the system
has changed both for the better
and the worse

A.L.

Dream

I want celebrity
to be a singer
a model
a good girl
but only in the sense
that good girls are bad girls
they just don't get caught

I want to be able to party
to dance, to have fun
drink Crystal
buy cars, houses
real Manolo Blahniks
I don't want to be the celebrity
that all Hollywood is gossiping about
because I go out
have mad girls in my house
and my clothes are tight
but if I am –
oh well
I don't care
I'd still be getting paid

but for now
I'm locked up
a good girl
in a bad girl

B.F.

Bridgeport Detention

my first night
I was alone
bored and cold
wanted to leave
cried myself to sleep
thought I was strong
but frozen inside
opened my eyes
saw the lights
shining bright
scary and hurt
just to know
I'm not alone
12 other girls
15 guys
on the right
only temporary
for the night
but even then
I didn't feel safe
for all I know
I could still get raped
even beat up
my first night
I kept to myself
didn't bother anyone
so they couldn't tell
well not on me
at the very least
let me be
I'm gonna sleep
it's my first night

Y.R.

Game of Life

It was a game at first –
challenging to play
but it got easier every day.

It was easy at times –
fooling at other times –
but I was never tricked.

It was about control
and I wasn't really happy
but then again, at the time, I was.

This game went on
and nothing stood in my way –
I liked to play it
and I was OK with the way it went.

It was fun for me
since I didn't care
but along the way people met me
and became part of my life –
part of this game.

From friend's houses to strange houses
I would stay – from detention to detention I would go –
it repeated itself and I would do anything
not to give up this thrilling game of life
I was really losing.

I learned the hurt the game was causing
when it was too late – I understand now
that this game I've learned to hate.

What to do to win this game?
Touchstone is helping find the way.

T.P.

Home?

What is it?
I long to find this.
But is it the ten thousand places I've lived
or just a word?
This makes me want to shout.
Is it heaven?
Is it hell?
Is it this earth?
I cannot tell.
Do I even have a home?
Do homes have doors and walls?
Do they have windows and furniture?
Or is home even a house?
Is it just the land we walk on,
the air we breathe,
the sidewalks we jog on?
Is it just a fictional place
where all dreams are forgotten?
Or is it a real place with your family and friends?
Is it the house where I live
or this horrible place I'm locked up in?
I guess I will never know exactly what home is
because no one wants to let me in!

H.J.

The Joy of Being Locked Up

yeah –
sounds kind of weird
but
it's a chance given to you
a chance nobody else would offer
a chance to change
to fix the things in need of fixing
to find you
not change you
to find you
start your life brand new
make sure what you're doing is true
not acting on all the crazy things
you would like to do
yeah –
I am trying to roam a world
I can't control
sometimes I think
I just want to smoke
but
we learned how to act and react
now we have goals that we can reach
now there's not so much pain and hurt
– at least not from the things
we have the power to change

so you see
it's not that bad
there is some joy
in being locked up
don't be so sad

D.R.D.

before submission

sometimes my past is kickin' my ass
'cuz I thought I was forced to sell crack
but that was part of the trap
the way they trapped me with
handcuffs cover-ups and bluffs
strip-searched in a cell
I was once closer steps to heaven than I fell
back in a cell
heart swelled with the reality
of misguidance and *I gotta eat*
I knew enough to be tough
knew too much before I knew
how to multiply and divide
I was adding and subtracting good and bad deeds
before I was even old enough for accountability
I counted how many times high in family's eyes
and friends said they would be there until the end
and I've seen the end
every time I had a friend
I knew too much before I knew
how to tie my shoes I was
dissin' shorties in preschool
'cuz they wasn't cool enough
to roll with my crew
sometimes I knew I was being fooled
but I had to do what I had to do to get through
till suddenly I knew
the hardest things to do is
submit completely to reality
my parents had managed to find
high-paying jobs with just a high school degree
and they was shaky mentally
the things I knew
shook my mind till I accepted them as fine
the way they took my crime
suppressed intellect unleash it in rhyme

and come to find
even my rhyme was crime
'cuz they was drunk and high
when I was rappin' about God they couldn't hear me
and they're still
drunk and high and can't hear me
and I'm still rhymin' about the crimes I used to do
tryin' to free my mind of what
I was fooled
and crying 'cuz
little over the age of nine
they got me drunk and high
asked me to forget about God and
just rap about crime
they didn't know
they was preparin' me for doing time
and it was during this time
that God I did find
while I was in a cold cell
I once was closer steps to hellfire
then I stepped it up
and I'm still steppin'

H.A.

What It's About Now

Mirror

when I look in the mirror
I see two sides of me
one side shows
the bright, happy proud and confident me
happy because I'm still here
still determined
proud because I've come this far by myself
confident because I am a beautiful young woman
who knows what she wants in life
and can hold her own

then there is the other side
the dark side
it shows all of the pain, the strife, the coldness
I've felt all my life
pain, because I've lost my mother
my family
to a drug
maybe not physically
but emotionally
strife, because I'm in the system
and can't get out
not due to me
but because I have no one
coldness, because of the shady men
who have come and gone

I've built a fortress
barricading my fragile heart
from any more emotion
that fortress has turned my insides cold

those are my reflections in the mirror
one shows the real me
one shows the cover up

A.L.

I Am a Woman Learning To Be Free

I am a woman learning to be free,
I want to be free as who I am
I want to learn from my mistakes,
learn yoga and meditation more.
I want to learn how to braid.
I want to be free.
I want to be able to identify words
so I can use them correctly
and in the right manner.
I want to learn about patience.
I want to learn from my wake-up calls.
I want to learn from the past,
learn about myself.

B.S.

What I Need

what I need
is a new life
I need to give
positive things a try
I need to stop
thinking about death
and relieve my stress
I need a happy family
instead of all the misery
they worry too much about stuff
I wish they would give it up
that's why I'm such a control freak
cause I was raised not to be lazy
I need to lose more weight
before it's too late
I need to go home with my mom
so she can live on
and have no more worries about me
and where I'm gonna be
I need to stop smoking
before I die from it
I need to relax
stop moving so fast
before I spazz out
I need my sister
to get her life right
because the stuff she be doing ain't right
she's older than me
but she is one of the dumbest people I know
it's a shame we have the same mother and father
I need to finish school
go to college and get a career
because the streets is fierce
nobody cares about what I need
but me

L.W.

need some thangz betta

if i could take back all my prior injustices
i would be justifiable
but i can't so where's da middle passage
tryin' to remain teachable to the morals of my tribulation
but my crescent moon is fallen from grace
my star is dim in its natural ability for greatness
when will i be free from the pain of my own thoughts
penetrating through a soul that could never be bought
self-taught
torn and born in da night where my secrecy sworn
searchin' for 20 degreez my vision through darkness
is reminiscent and not so prominent
not fearin' no man but fearin' self
confidence and the dominance of Allah
and his given power of chance in contrast
with my ability to further twist my future planz

H.A.

I've Learned That

I've learned that there's more to having tolerance
than how much you can smoke

that usually the right thing is the hardest

that I can love someone with all my heart
but it may not be healthy

that the things I don't like about others
are often the qualities I dislike about myself

that there comes a point where I can't justify
what I'm doing – then I know it's wrong

that I'm not invincible

that I won't let go yet
even though I will often

that the people who are good for you
are the ones who aren't afraid to tell you about yourself

that you'll always get caught, cause even if you didn't this time
you will next time

that everything happens for a reason
even if you never find out what it was

J.I.

What Would the World Look Like Without Violence?

If you ask me, the world would look like heaven.
There would be no drugs, no fights
and little girls would be able to ride their bikes.
Parents wouldn't have to worry if their kids
are going to make it home.
Communities won't have to pick up papers
and read about young kids getting shot at every day.
Is this place that fuckin' cold to where
they want to take a two-year old out of this world?

I think we could make it, but we have to try
and take it day by day, not year by year.
This world would not be like a shattered mirror
but more like a china cup. This world
without violence would be the best world
anyone could ever have.

S.C.

Change

It's a knot in my head that's tied real tight.
It seems to unravel in my mind when the time's just right.

It coats my spine with situations from the past.
Like a vine it curls around every bone.

With every crease there's a flower inpieced.
Full of things gone right, experiences well-learned.

As you look from my side you can see it's turned –
Coiling in my stomach, I begin to fill.

Full of hope, demand and fear – such simple, yet grand things.
I've grown to get to this day – it wasn't always this way.

J.I.

What It's About

it's not about where you are
it's where you're from

it's not about being fake to people
it's about being real to yourself

it's not about what people think of you
it's about what you think of you

it's not about what you show on the outside
it's what they don't see on the inside

it's not about the tears that show on my face
it's about the tears that no one sees

it's not about what I've said to you
it's about what you've done to me

it's not about you
it's about me

it's not about how far away we are
it's about how close we are together

it's not about what you've done in the past
it's what you're doing in the present

it's not about losing
it's about gaining

it's not about hate or love
it's not about us being lovers
it's about our friendship

it's not about falling
it's about getting back up

it's not about the loss
it's about the reproduction

it's not about death
it's about life!

A.L.

I Am Not a Juvenile Delinquent

I'm a child who's lost all hope.
I'm a piece of shattered glass –
An innocent soul corrupted by the world.
I'm a diamond that shines all the time.
I'm an angel gone bad.
My heart has armor on it.
If you took the time to look
you'd see it was split and fractured, needing to be stitched.
I'm a collection of cuts and bruises.
I cry so much but it relieves no stress.
I'm trapped in a glass jar, fermenting.
I have no father to guide me through this cold world.
I'm a miserable queen, so alone, so forgotten.
I have talents but they cannot find a home.
I have goals I want to reach.
I'm an addict.
My scars can tell the story.
My soul is like a see-through negligee.
I'm a victim of drugs, violence and hate.
I'm a failure in life.
I'm sweet and sour, taste me.
I am not the ideal daughter.
I'm a runaway.
I've been traumatized.
I'm an ace that gets played in the wrong game.
I scream in silence.
I am not what you think I am
but I am what you think I'm not.

How can I make you believe I am not a juvenile delinquent?
I've been tested and tried –
Look into my eyes.
See what I've seen.

girls of creative writing, winter 2004

Order More Copies

To obtain copies of this book, send a check for $15.00 made out to "Touchstone" for each copy plus $2.00 shipping/handling for your order to:

Sharon Charde
68 Reservoir Road
Lakeville, CT 06039

Include your name and address, the number of copies you are requesting, and specify *I Am Not a Juvenile Delinquent* as the book you are ordering. You can also email her at sharchar@mindspring.com for more information about anything concerning this book.

All monies from the sale of *I Am Not a Juvenile Delinquent* go into a fund that provides scholarship money for ex-residents and cultural and arts enrichment programs for the current girls.